GET REAL!

Snooping Snoopalot

by Phil Kettle

Illustrated by
Melissa Webb

Get Real!
Snooping Snoopalot

Written by Phil Kettle
Illustrations by Melissa Webb
Character design by David Dunstan

Text © 2009 Phil Kettle
Illustrations © 2009 Macmillan Education Australia Pty Ltd

All rights reserved. No part of this publication may be reproduced, stored in a retrieval system, or transmitted in any form or by any means, electronic, mechanical, photocopying, recording, or otherwise, without the prior permission of the copyright owner. While every care has been taken to trace and acknowledge copyright, the publishers tender their apologies for any accidental infringement where copyright has proved untraceable.

Published by
Macmillan Education Australia Pty Ltd
Level 1, 15–19 Claremont Street, South Yarra,
Victoria 3141
www.macmillan.com.au

Edited by Emma Short

Designed by Jenny Lindstedt,
Goanna Graphics (Vic) Pty Ltd

Printed in China
10 9 8 7 6 5 4 3 2

ISBN: (pack) 9781420278828

ISBN: 9781420277579

Contents

Introduction	5
Chapter One Extraordinary	7
Chapter Two An Opportunity	15
Chapter Three Meanwhile	22
Chapter Four Snoopalot	24
Chapter Five The Arrival	29
Chapter Six The Mission	32
Chapter Seven Back at the Park	37
Chapter Eight It Turned Out…	46
Chapter Nine Then	50
Chapter Ten Now	54
Chapter Eleven …and Then!	56
Let's Write	64
Harry and Jesse Present	66
Word-up!	68
A Laugh a Minute!	70

Introduction

The one standing on the left is Harry Harvard, but you already know that. And of course, if you know the one on the left is Harry, then you know that the one on the right is Jesse.

The one standing in between Harry and Jesse is Private Detective Snoopalot. You probably have absolutely no idea who Private Detective Snoopalot is, or why he's standing in between Harry and Jesse. But you will find out who Private Detective Snoopalot is when you read the rest of this story. SO GET ON WITH IT!

(If for some really strange reason, you decide that you don't want to read the rest of this story, then may I suggest you go and do something useful, like help your father wash the dishes!)

Chapter One

Extraordinary

Harry and Jesse were hurrying home to their tree house. It had been an extraordinarily strange day, even by the extraordinarily strange standards of the extraordinarily average students at Average Primary School.

> **AUTHOR NOTE**
> Wasn't that an extraordinarily long and confusing sentence?

Harry and Jesse were in a BIG hurry because they had a MAJOR problem. They needed to come up with a devious and dastardly plan. The only way Harry and Jesse could create a devious and dastardly plan was to be inspired. And nothing inspired them more than eating chips and peanut butter in their tree house.

A REMINDER FROM THE AUTHOR

I want to remind you that before this story started, something extraordinarily strange had happened in Average. If I don't remind you what happened, then nothing that happens in the rest of this story will make any sense, and you would be much better off helping your father take out the rubbish. (He's taking out the rubbish because he's finished washing the dishes. They're the dishes you didn't help him with, because you were busy reading the start of this story!)

SO WHAT HAPPENED IN AVERAGE THAT IS SO IMPORTANT TO THIS STORY?

During their school excursion to Big City Museum, Harry and Jesse saw a prehistoric caveman. (If you've read another story in this series, **Big City Museum**, you'll know what happened next.)

They used their time machine to travel back one million years in time. They arrived at Rocky Rockman's cave, picked up Rocky Rockman, and took him back to now time.

Later on, after they took Rocky Rockman to live in Average, Harry and Jesse went back one million years in time again to fetch his pet bird, Concorde. Back in Average, Rocky was totally excited that he was reunited with his best feathered friend.

Concorde was no average bird, but he soon became a favourite with everyone in Average — except Principal Dorking.

But that's another story. Actually it's not another story, it's part of this story, so keep reading...

Rocky had been very concerned about where Concorde was going to live. But nobody needed to have worried. Concorde had decided that he wanted to live in the best location in Average, and that was the top of the tallest tree in Average Park.

The next morning, all the mums and dads, kids and pets in Average Park were amazed to see a huge nest sitting on the top of the tallest tree.

"That's the second biggest nest I've ever seen!" said one mum to another.

While all the people in the park were staring at the nest on the top of the tree, a farmer in a nearby paddock was scratching his head and staring at a bare patch of ground. He was wondering where his haystack had gone!

Chapter Two

An Opportunity

As the days passed, more and more people arrived at the park. They all wanted to look at Concorde sitting in his nest on the top of the tree. Samantha Smithers recognised a good business opportunity when she saw one. She came up with a great idea to capitalise on the popularity of the prehistoric bird.

Average Daily News

A Great Idea

By Scoop Jones

Samantha Smithers, a Grade Six student at Average Primary School, has set up a Concorde Viewing Station in Average Park. Customers can watch Concorde the prehistoric bird while they enjoy a cup of lemonade.

"I see this as an opportunity for me to start a very successful business career. I intend one day to be the richest person in the world," said Samantha. I am particularly pleased that Harry Harvard will be working for me every day after school, and I'm even more pleased that he will be working for free."

When Jesse read that quote in the *Average Daily News*, he thought Harry must have gone totally mad.

Harry blushed and shrugged. "I guess I'd do anything for Sam," he said with a sigh.

Jesse just rolled his eyes.

Samantha Smithers wasn't the only one who came up with an idea. The Lord Mayor immediately saw a tourism opportunity for Average. He posted a message on the town website – www.average.notsogood.com.au.

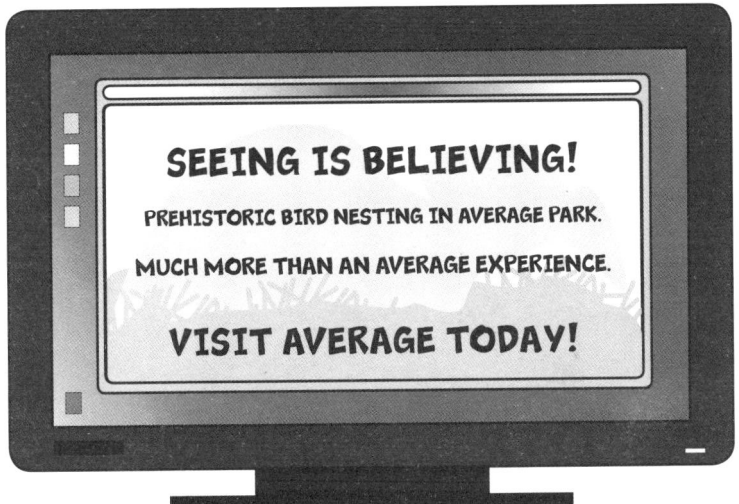

SEEING IS BELIEVING!

PREHISTORIC BIRD NESTING IN AVERAGE PARK.

MUCH MORE THAN AN AVERAGE EXPERIENCE.

VISIT AVERAGE TODAY!

People from all over the world responded to the message. Within a matter of days, bus loads of tourists started to arrive in Average.

Chapter Three

Meanwhile

While most of Average was abuzz with excitement, Principal Dorking was anything but abuzz with excitement. He was simply pacing around his desk and talking to himself.

"I'm going to find out about all the strange things that Harvard and Harrison have been up to. And then I'm going to expel them – and maybe the rest of Grade Five too."

Principal Dorking walked around his desk six hundred and thirty-three times. Then he came up with a brilliant idea that would allow him to get rid of Harry and Jesse – and maybe the rest of Grade Five too – FOREVER.

Chapter four

Snoopalot

Principal Dorking sat down at his desk, opened a drawer and took out a small black book. He flicked through it until he found a certain telephone number.

"Private Detective Snoopalot," he grinned. "He's my man!"

BRRRIIING BRRRIIING

"Snoopalot speaking. The effective detective who's far from defective."

"Principal Dorking here, Snoopalot. From Average Primary School."

"How can I help you Dorking?"

"Have you got any references?"

"Well, Mrs Smithers employed me to find her lost cat. I snooped and sneaked until I eventually found her cat."

"So Snoopalot, how and where did you find Mrs Smithers' cat?"

"I sneaked and snooped and I looked up into a tree, and there was Mrs Smithers' cat."

"In a tree? What made you look up in the tree?"

"The cat was meowing."

"So, how did you get the cat out of the tree?"

"That's good enough for me, Mr Snoopalot," declared Principal Dorking. "How long before you can be in Average?"

"I'll be there tomorrow."

Chapter five

The Arrival

The next evening, Private Detective Snoopalot snuck into Average under the cover of darkness. Moments after he arrived, he rushed to Principal Dorking's office. Principal Dorking told Private Detective Snoopalot that he was required to swear an oath of allegiance.

After Private Detective Snoopalot had sworn the oath of allegiance, Principal Dorking outlined the mission.

"Your mission, Mr Snoopalot, if you choose to accept it, is to snoop, sneak and find out all that there is to be found out about Jesse Harrison and Harry Harvard, and their devious and dastardly plans. I need to know everything there is to know about their tricks and their secrets too."

"Principal Dorking," Private Detective Snoopalot replied in a serious tone. "This is an incredibly dangerous mission. I could be risking my life, BUT this is a mission that has my name written all over it."

Chapter Six

The Mission

Private Detective Snoopalot immediately embarked on his mission. This meant that he started snooping and sneaking straight away. In fact, he snooped and sneaked into parts of Average that nobody had ever snooped and sneaked in before.

While Private Detective Snoopalot was snooping and sneaking around Average, Principal Dorking was relaxing in his office. He was feeling particularly pleased with himself.

"Dorking, not only are you a truly handsome and incredible human being, you are also brilliant and super-intelligent," said Principal Dorking to himself. "Soon you'll be rid of Harry Harvard and Jesse Harrison – and maybe the rest of Grade Five – FOREVER. And when you get rid of them, you'll get rid of that freaky caveman and that scary prehistoric bird that's living in Average Park, too."

Principal Dorking smiled and waved at himself in the mirror before he sat back down at his desk. But he wouldn't have been anywhere near as happy with himself if he had known what Harry and Jesse were up to. For at that very moment, they were sitting in their tree house, trying to come up with inspiration for another devious and dastardly plan.

A NOTE FROM THE AUTHOR

And that takes us back to the beginning of our story. Harry and Jesse were trying to come up with a devious and dastardly plan because they already knew all about Private Detective Snoopalot's mission. HOW did they know about Private Detective Snoopalot's mission? Because of the secret spy microphones that they had secretly planted in Principal Dorking's office the last time they were called in there.

"So Harry," said Jesse, gobbling down another handful of chips. "It's US against THEM."

"Actually," Harry chuckled, reaching for the peanut butter. "It's US PLUS OUR TIME MACHINE PLUS ROCKY AND CONCORDE against THEM."

Jesse and Harry glanced at each other. Nothing else needed to be said. Faster than a mean primary school principal can call up a defective private detective, Harry and Jesse raced off on their skateboards to Average Park.

Chapter Seven

Back at the Park

Harry and Jesse knew they had to stop Private Detective Snoopalot from snooping, sneaking and finding out anything that Principal Dorking might use against them. But maybe it was too late. Private Detective Snoopalot had already been doing a lot of snooping and sneaking and had found out important new information about prehistoric birds.

Never stand under a giant prehistoric bird's nest.

Rocky was already at the park. When he saw Harry and Jesse, he ran towards them as fast as he could.

> ### A REMINDER FROM THE AUTHOR
> Just in case you've forgotten, Rocky was an awesomely fast runner. This was because in prehistoric time, he was always running away from fearsomely large, man-eating prehistoric animals!

"I'm really excited," Rocky shouted, waving his hands wildly. "And I have some really great news!"

"And what would that really great news be?" asked Harry.

"Well," said Rocky, huffing and puffing as he pulled up next to Harry and Jesse. "Concorde's not a *he*, he's a *she*!"

"What do mean, Rocky?" asked Jesse.

"Well, unless I'm mistaken, male birds don't lay eggs. But Concorde has laid an egg in his new nest. He's going to be a MOTHER!" Rocky yelled.

"No Rocky, *she's* going to be a mother," laughed Harry.

"And we're going to have another prehistoric monster bird flying around Average," winked Jesse.

Just then, Private Detective Snoopalot, who had been snooping and sneaking around Average Park, overheard Rocky tell Harry and Jesse that Concorde had laid an egg in the nest. He immediately pulled his phone out of his pocket and called Principal Dorking.

"Dorking, this is Snoopalot."

"Snoopalot, what have you got for me?"

"Nothing – is it your birthday? Because if you want me to buy you a present, then you'll have to pay me more money."

"It's not my birthday," Principal Dorking growled. "I mean 'do you have any information'?"

"Ah yes," replied Private Detective Snoopalot. "I have some very important information – information that only a skilled investigator like me could obtain."

"And what's that?" Principal Dorking asked.

"There's an egg in the nest!" announced Private Detective Snoopalot with glee. "A huge egg! And that means another huge prehistoric bird flying around Average with its mother!"

Principal Dorking had been sitting at his desk, dreaming about how great it would be at Average Primary School when he finally expelled Harry and Jesse. On hearing the news about the egg, he became even more excited than when he nominated himself for the International Primary School Principal of the Year award. (Then he remembered how disappointed he felt when he was disqualified for nominating himself.)

"Snoopalot, I WANT THAT EGG!" Principal Dorking shouted into the phone.

"Hmmm," said Jesse to Harry and Rocky. "This is going to be BIG news for Principal Dorking."

"Agreed," nodded Harry. "The only way we can stop Principal Dorking and the defective detective, is to work out exactly what they are going to do *before* they do it."

"Just as well we know exactly how we can do that," replied Jesse. He pulled out the remote control for the time machine and programmed their destination.

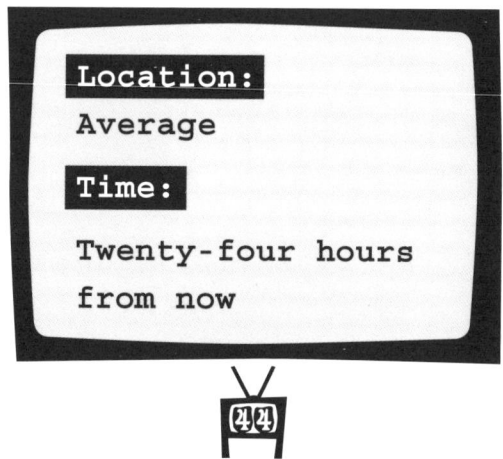

Location:
Average

Time:
Twenty-four hours from now

"Ready Harry?"

"Ready Jesse!"

"One...*two*...THREE!"

Together they pressed the red button on the remote control to activate the time machine. And faster than Rocky Rockman could outrun a very hungry woolly mammoth, Harry and Jesse found themselves sitting in Principal Dorking's office, and in BIG trouble.

A NOTE FROM THE AUTHOR

Why were Harry and Jesse in **BIG** trouble? Because of everything that happens in the next two chapters, of course...

Chapter eight

It Turned Out...

...that a massive crowd had gathered in Average Park that afternoon to look at the egg in Concorde's nest. Everyone was wondering when the egg would hatch. Private Detective Snoopalot sent Principal Dorking a photo from his mobile phone to show him the size of the egg.

Principal Dorking logged on to his computer and found an online auction site. He uploaded the picture of the egg.

Meanwhile, the massive crowd in Average Park continued to grow. Samantha Smithers sold more lemonade than she'd ever imagined anyone would want to drink – except perhaps Lenny 'the Stink' Edwards. And Lenny 'the Stink' Edwards drank more lemonade than he'd ever imagined anyone would want to sell – except perhaps Samantha Smithers.

Chapter Nine

Then

While everyone was busy down at the park, Private Detective Snoopalot snuck into Harry and Jesse's tree house and snooped around inside it. He found something that looked like a very old television, but Private Detective Snoopalot wasn't fooled.

"Unless I'm very much mistaken, that's a time machine!"

Detective Snoopalot took the television that looked like a time machine to Principal Dorking's office. When Principal Dorking saw it, he got more excited than ever. "Now I know why all these strange things have been happening in Average. It must be because of this time machine!"

Principal Dorking tried to make the time machine work by pressing some buttons and switches, but nothing happened. Then he went back to his computer and checked for bids on the egg. The highest bid was for one million dollars! Principal Dorking danced around his office desk.

The next morning, Principal Dorking made an announcement at assembly. He told all the staff and students to take the rest of the week off – except Harry and Jesse.

Everybody cheered. Mrs Payne said it was the best day in the history of Average Primary School. Mrs McBurger, the canteen manager, said, "What am I going to do with all the food in the canteen?"

Lenny 'the Stink' Edwards said that he would help Mrs McBurger get rid of it.

After assembly, everyone went home. Principal Dorking called Harry and Jesse to his office. And that is where Harry and Jesse found themselves in BIG trouble.

Chapter Ten

Now

Principal Dorking smiled at Harry and Jesse.

"I've got you NOW!" he smirked.

Harry and Jesse smiled back at Principal Dorking.

"You haven't got us at all," Jesse explained. "Because in a moment, NOW will be gone. And when NOW is gone, you won't remember THEN."

Jesse reached into his back pocket and pressed the blue button on the remote control for the time machine. And faster than Principal Dorking could work out if NOW was THEN or THEN was NOW, Harry and Jesse whirled back through time and into their tree house.

Chapter eleven

...and Then!

The boys found themselves back in Average Park and saw Private Detective Snoopalot snooping and sneaking about. He was just about to call Principal Dorking with the news about Concorde's egg.

"Hey Snoopalot," yelled Harry. "Mrs Smithers has lost her cat again. She needs you to find it right away!"

Snoopalot picked up his phone and called Principal Dorking.

"Principal Dorking here, Average Primary School."

"Principal Dorking. It's Private Detective Snoopalot here."

"Snoopalot. What's up?"

"There's an emergency."

"What kind of emergency? Does it have anything to do with Harvard and Harrison?"

"Well no. Actually this emergency has nothing to do with my mission."

"Please explain, Private Detective Snoopalot."

"Mrs Smithers has lost her cat again."

"That's terrible. But so what?"

"She needs the skills of an effective detective who's far from defective. I'm off!"

"Private Detective Snoopalot, you're FIRED!"

"See you later, Snoopalot!" called Jesse, as Private Detective Snooplot snuck off through the trees in Average Park.

"That's the last we'll see of him for a while," laughed Harry. "Now Concorde's egg is safe – and so is our time machine!"

Just then, Jesse heard a small cracking sound.   CRACK

"Hey Harry, did you hear that?"

"What?"   CRACK

"That!"

"No, I didn't hear anything."   **CRACK**

"Hmmm, what about that?" asked Jesse.

"Yes, I think I heard that," said Harry.

Jesse and Harry looked up.   CRACK

"Concorde's egg is about to hatch!" they shouted together.

CRACK

Average Daily News

Baby Bird Born in Average Park

By Scoop Jones

A new baby bird arrived in Average today. The giant egg of Concorde the prehistoric bird finally hatched. Everybody in the park was very excited, especially Rocky Rockman.

"I'm a grandfather!" he said. "Meet my new grandbird. His name is Jet!"

Let's Write

Overcoming an obstacle

A writing adventure can be a lot like a real-life adventure. Sometimes things happen that may cause you to change your direction or plan. The same can happen during your writing adventure. You might run into an obstacle that causes you to change direction in your story.

I don't think you need to plan a complication. I just think you should enjoy your writing adventure. But of course, when you come to an obstacle, you might need to figure out how to overcome it. Consider those obstacles a part of the writing adventure!

My story plan – obstacles

Use your imagination and pretend that you're going on an adventure into the largest and wildest jungle in the entire world. As you are going through the jungle, you come across a huge lion. You need to get to the other side of the jungle and the only thing stopping you is that lion.

The lion is your obstacle. How do you get past it? Write down all the ways that you can overcome this obstacle. And remember, complications are just another part of the writing adventure!

Harry and Jesse Present

About the Author

Harry: Phil, you told me that ideas for stories come from three sources.

Phil: That's right – from things you've seen, things you've heard and things you've done.

Harry: Um, Phil, I really don't think you would have ever seen or done much of what you've written in this story. So I think it must have come from something you heard about.

Phil: True! Most of the ideas for this story came from listening to a program on the radio called No Holiday for Halliday, when I was young. Lots of strange things happened in that radio show.

Harry: So all I need to do to write a great story is listen to the radio?

Phil: Sort of. But you also need imagination and inspiration – and that's how I created this story.

About the Illustrator

Harry: Hey Melissa, would you like to be a private detective?

Melissa: Oh yes, I am very nosey.

Harry: And have you ever seen a baby bird hatch from an egg?

Melissa: Yes, I have seen chicks hatching from eggs at the Royal Melbourne Show. I highly recommend it!

Word-up!

Precaution: something you get before a caution

Nightrise: what happens before the nightfall

Kidnapping: what little kids do after lunch

Overjoyed: people who are way too happy

Sunfall: what happens after the sunrise

A Laugh a Minute!

What do you call an American drawing?
A yankee doodle!

Why did the boy take a pencil to bed?
To draw the curtains!

Why did the burglar take a shower?
To make a clean get-away!

What is hairy and coughs a lot?
A coconut with a sore throat!

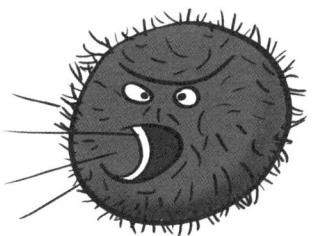

What did the necktie say to the hat?
I'll hang around here while you go on ahead!

What did the painting say to the wall?
I've got you covered!

Other Titles in the Series

The Time Machine

Ferret Attack

The Trouble with...

Just Another Day

Planet Snoz

Big City Museum

The Flying Machines

The Pirate Play

The Last Day